Pebble™ Plus

A Visit to

The Fire Station

by B. A. Hoena

Consulting Editor: Gail Saunders-Smith, Ph.D.
Reading Consultant: Jennifer Norford, Senior Consultant
Mid-continent Research for Education and Learning
Aurora, Colorado

Capstone press

Mankato, Minnesota

Pebble Plus is published by Capstone Press
151 Good Counsel Drive, P.O. Box 669, Mankato, Minnesota 56002
www.capstonepress.com

1 2 3 4 5 6 09 08 07 06 05 04

Library of Congress Cataloging-in-Publication Data
Hoena, B. A.
 The fire station/by B. A. Hoena.
 p. cm.—(Pebble Plus, A visit to)
 Includes bibliographical references and index.
 Contents: The fire station—Trucks and gear—Around the fire station—Working together.
 ISBN 0-7368-2392-1 (hardcover)
 1. Fire stations—Juvenile literature. [1. Fire stations.] 1. Title. II. Series.
TH9148.H67 2004
628.9'25—dc22   2003011992

Editorial Credits
Sarah L. Schuette, editor; Jennifer Bergstrom, series designer; Karen Risch, product planning editor

Photo Credits
Capstone Press/Gary Sundermeyer, all

Pebble Plus thanks the New Ulm Fire Department, New Ulm, Minnesota, for the use of its
department during photo shoots.

Note to Parents and Teachers

The series A Visit to supports national social studies standards related to the production,
distribution, and consumption of goods and services. This book describes and illustrates
a visit to a fire station. The images support early readers in understanding the text. The
repetition of words and phrases helps early readers learn new words. This book also
introduces early readers to subject-specific vocabulary words, which are defined in the
Glossary section. Early readers may need assistance to read some words and to use the
Table of Contents, Glossary, Read More, Internet Sites, and Index/Word List sections of
the book.

Word Count: 123
Early-Intervention Level: 13

Table of Contents

The Fire Station

A fire station is a fun

place to visit.

Trucks and Gear

Fire engines have flashing
lights and loud horns.
Fire engines and other trucks
park in the bay.

Some fire trucks carry
ladders. Ladders can reach
the tops of tall buildings.

Firefighters wear coats,
helmets, and boots.
The heavy gear keeps
them safe.

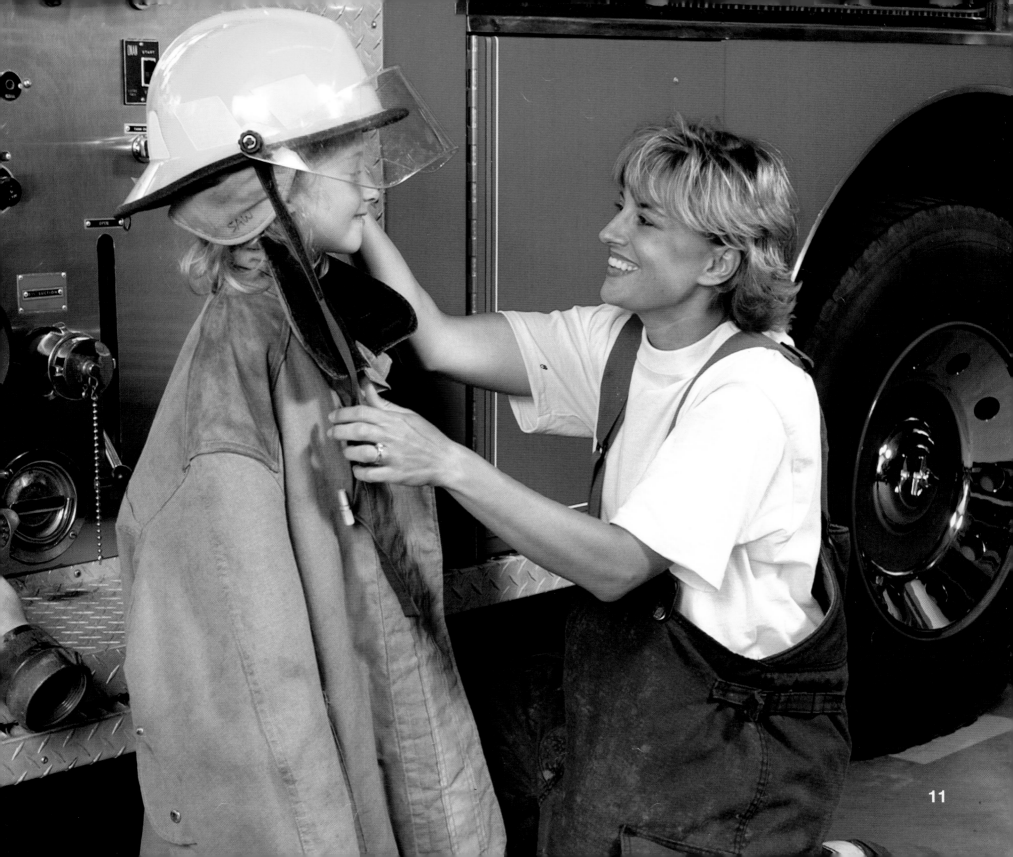

Around the Fire Station

Dispatchers tell firefighters
how to get to a fire quickly.
Dispatchers listen to radios,
read maps, and answer calls.

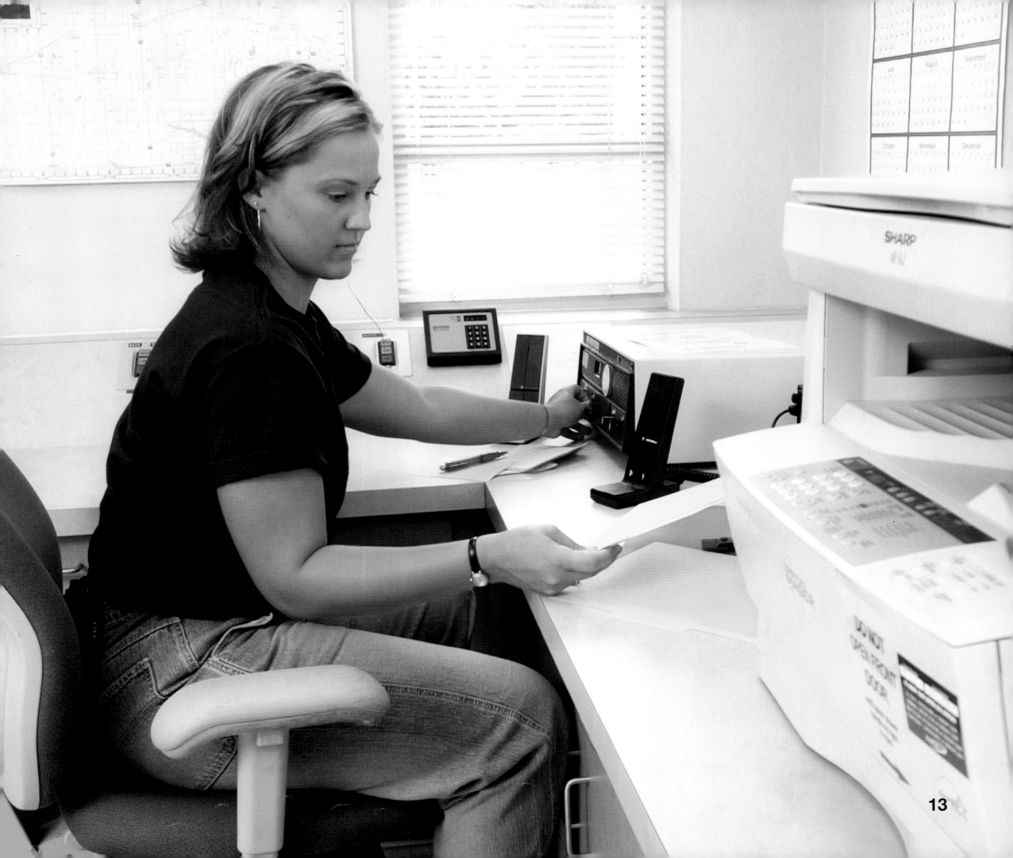

Firefighters learn in the training room. They hear and see how to use new safety equipment.

Firefighters exercise in
the dorm during the day.
They rest in beds at night.

Firefighters cook meals
in the kitchen. They
eat together during breaks.

Working Together

People at the fire station work together to keep their community safe.

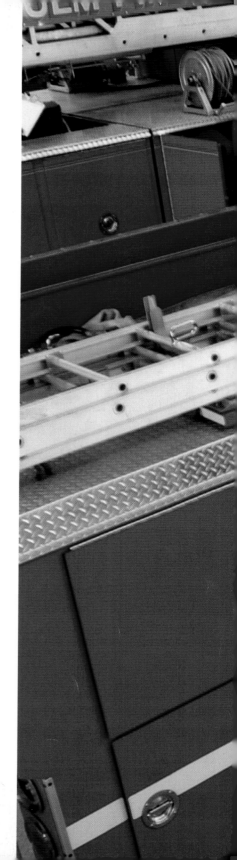

Glossary

bay—the area in a fire station where trucks and other firefighting equipment is kept; the bay is on the ground floor so that trucks can drive onto the street.

dorm—a room or a building with beds; another word for dorm is dormitory.

fire engine—a large truck that carries firefighting equipment to a fire; firefighters also ride on fire engines.

gear—a set of clothing or equipment; firefighters wear heavy coats, pants, and boots called bunker gear.

truck—a vehicle; fire stations use many different kinds of trucks; pumper trucks carry and pump water; ladder trucks carry tall ladders to fires.

Read More

Canizares, Susan. *Firehouse.* New York: Scholastic, 2000.

Dubois, Muriel L. *Out and About at the Fire Station.* Minneapolis: Picture Window Books, 2003.

Gorman, Jacqueline Laks. *Firefighter.* People in My Community. Milwaukee: Weekly Reader Early Learning Library, 2002.

Internet Sites

FactHound offers a safe, fun way to find Internet sites related to this book. All of the sites on FactHound have been researched by our staff.

Here's how:

1. Visit *www.facthound.com*

2. Type in this special code **0736823921** for age-appropriate sites. Or enter a search word related to this book for a more general search.

3. Click on the Fetch It button.

FactHound will fetch the best sites for you!

Index/Word List